T0129739

Finding a Church Home

Michael E. Stertz

WESTBOW
PRESS®
A DIVISION OF THOMAS NELSON
& ZONDERVAN

WestBow Press books may be ordered through booksellers or by contacting:

WestBow Press
A Division of Thomas Nelson & Zondervan
1663 Liberty Drive
Bloomington, IN 47403
www.westbowpress.com
1 (866) 928-1240

ISBN: 978-1-9736-4323-4 (sc)
ISBN: 978-1-9736-4324-1 (e)

Library of Congress Control Number: 2018912479

Print information available on the last page.

WestBow Press rev. date: 10/24/2018

Contents

CHAPTER 1

The Issue

Every Christian needs to be involved in a local church. This can be a bigger challenge than it might seem. Perhaps you have struggled to find the right church for you and your family after you have moved to a different area. Maybe you were discouraged by a bad experience with a church in the past or you simply dropped out of church. Now you have made the decision that you want to go back to church and need to find a church to attend. Possibly you have become concerned that the church you attend falls short or doesn't meet your needs or the needs of your family, or maybe it has drifted from a proper foundation. A new pastor is taking the church in a direction you do not want to go. Often what passes for "church" in twenty-first-century America isn't what the New Testament presents to us. In most American communities, there are several churches. How does one find the "right" congregation? What makes for a healthy church?

As a conservative, Bible-believing evangelical, I am committed to the necessity of believers being involved with a community of like-minded followers of Christ in a church. I have been an active, committed member of local churches all my life. Often, I've struggled with mediocrity, failure, and error in those churches. Family, tradition, friends, and long-term relationships make it difficult to consider leaving, and the process of visiting and evaluating another church can be an intimidating task. My hope is that if you find yourself in such a situation that you will find this writing helpful.

It is also my hope to challenge churches to evaluate their ministries. Church leaders need to ask themselves not only why someone would want to attend the church they lead but why should someone attend. What effect does the church have on the people who attend? Are people being discipled, and are people growing in their faith? Does your church truly serve and worship the Lord? Is there a manifestation of the New Testament gifts of the Spirit in ministry? Are people coming to faith through the ministry of the church and its members? What impact does the church have on people in the community in which its members live? Or is your church just going through the motions? Does the church just drift along while decline and erosion happen? Why do you do what you do, and why do you do things the way you do? Above all, does your church stand committed to the truth of Scripture? A church that is not consciously and continuously evaluated may not be worth attending or supporting.

I will focus attention on two central areas of teaching, not because they are the only important doctrines but because they are the foundational essentials and the most telling teachings in the evaluation of a local church. If a church gets it right in these two areas, it will likely be solid in other essential beliefs as well. Further, I will discuss the leadership of the church and the impact the church has on the lives of its members. Finally, I will discuss other characteristics that are not essential beliefs but nevertheless will be necessary considerations.

CHAPTER 2

What Is a Church?

I once had lunch with a somewhat disgruntled member of the small church we attended. He said that if one looked at the church financial statements and the activities of the church (he was an accountant by profession, and I was a deacon in this church), one could easily conclude that the church existed primarily to raise funds to pay the pastor and secretary. I couldn't argue with him. The church met for weekly services and collected an offering. There were small groups that met during the week. Some funds were sent to missionaries serving in various mission fields, but locally, little happened in the life of this church. The services were forgettable, with no spirit of worship and preaching that lacked both impact and real examination of Scripture. Occasionally, someone joined the church, someone left the church, or an attender died, and the attendance just slowly declined over time. Seldom was there evidence of anyone coming to faith through the ministry of the church or the efforts of the members, and almost never was anyone baptized. That church has a correct, orthodox doctrinal statement with a group of people who genuinely love Christ and love each other's fellowship. But that church was and remains essentially dead.

It is important to commit to a church that is alive and will benefit you and your family. Consider carefully how the ministry of the church can bring spiritual growth. But don't make it all about you. Think about how you might serve if you became a part of the church, observing how the church moves its congregation to be involved in bringing people to faith and then discipling them. And remember that the church is ultimately not just about you, the congregation, or the community. It is the body of Christ and worshipping God and bringing glory to Him is the highest goal of a church. Professor Robert L. Saucy wrote,

> Worship is central in the existence of the church. The words of the apostle Paul that God has chosen and predestined sons unto Himself in Christ "to the praise of the glory of his grace" (Eph 1:4–6) suggest that the ultimate purpose of the church is the worship of the one who called it into being.[1]

He expands on this idea of worship in the church, noting the three words in the original language that are the most often translated "worship." The first word denotes "the act of bowing or prostrating oneself in submissive lowliness and

---

[1] Robert L. Saucy, *The Church in God's Program.* (Chicago, IL, Moody Press, 1972), 166.

deep reverence" with "the inward attitude of submission and humble respect." The second word indicates "reverence which stresses the feeling of awe." And the third is a "total manner of life which is pleasing to God."[2] The weekly meetings of the congregation should include approaching God with a spirit of reverence and awe, with a view toward preparing worshippers to live a life pleasing to God.

What is a church? In the New Testament, the church is identified by several metaphors, including family, bride, vineyard, temple, building, kingdom, flock, and body. The church is a communion, a fellowship, an assembly of believers called out from the world as a new and separate entity, and a local, visible group. Saucy wrote,

> As for membership in an invisible church without fellowship with any local assembly, this concept is never contemplated in the New Testament. The universal church was the universal fellowship of believers who met visibly in local assemblies.[3]

I once saw a church slogan that included the phrase, "Belong before you believe." Nothing could be further from the New Testament teaching concerning the church. Visitors should be warmly welcomed and actively encouraged to attend public services, but no attender can belong to a church until he or she has come to faith and publicly identifies with the

---

[2] Ibid., 167.
[3] Ibid., 17.

church as a baptized believer. A church is composed of a group of baptized believers who are associated by their common commitment in faith and fellowship around the gospel. They observe the two ordinances of baptism and communion, are committed to the teaching of Scripture, seek to fellowship, grow together, and share the gospel with unbelievers. It is not just a group of people with some sort of religious interest but an assembly of people who believe in Jesus Christ as Savior and Lord.

A church is governed and organized according to principles laid out in the New Testament. More than a club or organization, it is a spiritual organism. First Corinthians 12 explains that the church is a body composed of many parts, with all actively functioning together in a loving relationship. A church should be alive. It should be a community of believers who encourage each other, love each other, serve each other, and are committed to the task of knowing, loving, and serving God together. Discipleship and spiritual growth will be evident in a healthy church.

The local church has three elements to its purpose and mission. The church is God's program to reach people with the message of salvation. Evangelism—reaching lost people with the gospel—is essential and happens in a variety of ways. But the mission goes far beyond that. Furthermore, evangelism is an outgrowth of the two other elements of the church's purpose. The church has a mission to itself: to develop its members in life and faith. Ephesians 4:11–16 tells us,

And He Himself gave some *to be* apostles, some prophets, some evangelists, and some pastors and teachers, for the equipping of the saints for the work of ministry, for the edifying of the body of Christ, till we all come to the unity of the faith and of the knowledge of the Son of God, to a perfect man, to the measure of the stature of the fullness of Christ; that we should no longer be children, tossed to and fro and carried about with every wind of doctrine, by the trickery of men, in the cunning craftiness of deceitful plotting, but, speaking the truth in love, may grow up in all things into Him who is the head—Christ—from whom the whole body, joined and knit together by what every joint supplies, according to the effective working by which every part does its share, causes growth of the body for the edifying of itself in love.

The church is gifted with those who are to lead the congregation and minister to the people to build the people in faith. Jude 20–21 says,

But you, beloved, building yourselves up on your most holy faith, praying in the Holy Spirit, keep yourselves in the love of God, looking for the mercy of our Lord Jesus Christ unto eternal life.

Believers are to always be in the process of becoming stronger and more mature in their faith, and the church is to help them in that growth process.

Corporate worship builds up the body of Christ and should be central to the gathering of the church. The New Testament shows us several elements that should be present when the church gathers to worship. Reading Scripture and preaching Scripture are to be a dominant focus. Actively considering the Word together as it is taught and preached is an act of worship for the congregation. The sermon is the central element of the service, and the sermon should focus on the Scripture. Paul wrote in Colossians 3:16, "Let the Word of Christ dwell in you richly in all wisdom, teaching and admonishing one another in psalms and hymns and spiritual songs, singing with grace in your hearts to the Lord" and in Ephesians 5:18–19, "And do not be drunk with wine, in which is dissipation; but be filled with the Spirit, speaking to one another in psalms and hymns and spiritual songs, singing and making melody in your heart to the Lord." People in a church admonish one another and build each other up in the faith as we sing to the Lord, and as we praise God, we express our hearts in worship to Him. Music becomes an act of worship when the words of that music celebrate God, His nature, His attributes, and what Christ has done for us. Praying (1 Timothy 2:1–2, 8) should not be limited to a quick, "Now I lay me down to sleep" prayer or a muttered few phrases as a prayer to open the service. Real prayer, both public and offered privately by the congregants, is important. Baptism and the Lord's

Supper, or Communion, are to be practiced by a church (Matthew 28:19, 1 Corinthians 11:17–34). They are not done as rites leading to salvation, since salvation comes only through faith in Christ, but they are not optional and will be practiced in a healthy church, and the church should provide a clear explanation of these ordinances and show a high regard for them. Communion as a memorial of the sacrifice of Christ should be practiced in a deeply respectful and appropriate manner as the congregation remembers Christ and His sacrifice as pictured in the communion elements. New believers being baptized should be able to give credible testimony of faith in Christ. Hebrews 10:24–25 speaks of moving one another to love and good deeds, and one way that happens is when the church gathers for corporate worship. Paul goes so far as to say that *everything* in the gathered assembly should be done with a view to building up the body in Christ (1 Corinthians 14:26).

> Yet Scripture's goal for a church's public gatherings should be different: not entertainment, but exposure to God's Word. Churches are told to preach the Word, sing the Word, read the Word, portray the gospel Word through the ordinances, and build one another up with words (see 1 Cor. 11, 14; Eph. 4; Col. 3; 2 Tim. 4).[4]

---

[4] Jonathan Leeman, *Word Centered Church*. (Chicago, IL, Moody Publishers, 2017), 77.

Ultimately, the mission of the church is to glorify God and His Son. Church gatherings should be God-centered.

> The primary end of coming together as a body of believers is Godward in praise and adoration and then toward itself in edification as the various ministries of the Spirit are manifest, especially the preaching and teaching of the Word. Nevertheless, the congregational meeting also serves as a witness to the world. The true manifestation of God's presence in the church cannot be avoided by the unbelievers who are present, with the result that at least some will worship God (I Co 14:23-25).[5]

Ephesians 3:21 tells us "to Him *be* glory in the church by Christ Jesus to all generations, forever and ever." Evangelism does not occur just through formal evangelistic efforts or entertaining events directed toward unbelievers. Believers do not become mature in their faith merely through academic exercises, but the mission of the church will only be fulfilled when believers are challenged and equipped to effectively live out their relationship with Christ. The church gathers together to grow in faith and knowledge and to worship God as a community.

A consideration of a church's beliefs and teaching perspective is of utmost importance when evaluating the church. Unfortunately, there is not universal agreement on

---

[5] Saucy, 93.

this. Some would say that community is more important than doctrine, or would argue that Christianity is a life, not a system of doctrine, and building relationships is what is important. Others would emphasize experience and feeling or would say that truth is, after all, a subjective concept. But Scripture knows nothing of relative truth. An examination of the New Testament will indicate the importance of doctrine, and a true Christian church will be openly doctrinal.

In 2 Timothy 3:16–17 we read,

> All Scripture *is* given by inspiration of God, and *is* profitable for doctrine, for reproof, for correction, for instruction in righteousness, that the man of God may be complete, thoroughly equipped for every good work.

Acts 5:28 indicates the charge of their enemies that the early disciples had "filled Jerusalem with your doctrine." The apostle Paul repeatedly exhorted the teaching of doctrine. Note his instructions to Timothy in 1 Timothy 4:6: "If you instruct the brethren in these things, you will be a good minister of Jesus Christ, nourished in the words of faith and of the good doctrine which you have carefully followed." Again in 2 Timothy 4:2–4, Paul wrote,

> Preach the word! Be ready in season *and* out of season. Convince, rebuke, exhort, with all longsuffering and teaching. For the time will come when they will not endure sound

doctrine, but according to their own desires, *because* they have itching ears, they will heap up for themselves teachers; and they will turn *their* ears away from the truth, and be turned aside to fables.

In Titus 1:9, we read Paul's instruction to Titus concerning an elder, "holding fast the faithful word as he has been taught, that he may be able, by sound doctrine, both to exhort and convict those who contradict."

Constantly teaching doctrine is necessary to communicate, defend, and preserve the faith. In Philippians 1:27, we read "Only let your conduct be worthy of the gospel of Christ, so that whether I come and see you or am absent, I may hear of your affairs, that you stand fast in one spirit, with one mind striving together for the faith of the gospel." We are told to "contend" for the faith. Jude 3 tells us, "Beloved, while I was very diligent to write to you concerning our common salvation, I found it necessary to write to you exhorting you to contend earnestly for the faith which was once for all delivered to the saints." We are instructed to know how to answer questions concerning our faith. Colossians 4:6 reads, "*Let* your speech always *be* with grace, seasoned with salt, that you may know how you ought to answer each one." A church should not be so much a witness to inner experience but to the objective truth about Christ and redemption. Members in a church need to be growing in their understanding of the Scriptures.

Philippians 1:9–11 tells us,

> And this I pray, that your love may abound still more and more in knowledge and all discernment, that you may approve the things that are excellent, that you may be sincere and without offense till the day of Christ, being filled with the fruits of righteousness which *are* by Jesus Christ, to the glory and praise of God.

The passage tells believers to grow in knowledge and depth of wisdom and understanding so we can begin to make wise decisions. Your consideration of a church will necessitate the exercise of wisdom and discernment. Ask questions. Pray diligently. James 1:5 tells us, "If any of you lacks wisdom, let him ask of God, who gives to all liberally and without reproach, and it will be given to him." Do not expect a dream, vision, or voice from heaven, but consider Scripture and use wisdom and discernment to carefully evaluate your options and prayerfully commit to finding the right church family.

CHAPTER 3

The Church and the Bible

The grass withers, the flower fades, But the word of our God stands forever.

—Isaiah 40:8

The great disaster in the wake of rationalism, liberalism, and modernism in the nineteenth and twentieth centuries left a huge segment of Christendom that does not believe the Scriptures to be the Word of God. Most Protestant and denominational churches no longer hold to the inspiration and authority of the Bible. As a result, these churches have lost any distinctively Christian message and have become irrelevant as they have drifted away from the faith. With no distinct message or purpose, people are no longer attracted to those churches. Western Europe is almost devoid of a true Christian witness, and liberal churches in North America have greatly declined in membership. In 1984 American theologian Francis Schaeffer warned that the evangelical church had also lost a strong view of Scripture:

Here is the great evangelical disaster—the failure of the evangelical world to stand for truth as truth. There is only one word for this—namely *accommodation:* the evangelical church has accommodated to the world spirit of the age. First, there has been accommodation on Scripture, so that many who call themselves evangelicals hold a weakened view of the Bible and no longer affirm the truth of all the Bible teaches—truth not only in religious matters but in the areas of science and history and morality. As part of this, many evangelicals are now accepting the higher critical methods in the study of the Bible. Remember, it was these same methods which destroyed the authority for the Protestant church in Germany in the last century, and which have destroyed the Bible for the liberal in our own country from the beginning of this century. And second, there has been accommodation on the issues, with no clear stand being taken even on matters of life and death.[6]

Further, Schaeffer wrote,

Within evangelicalism there is a growing number who are modifying their views on the

---

[6] Francis A. Schaeffer, *The Great Evangelical Disaster.* (Westchester, IL: Crossway Books, 1984), 37.

inerrancy of the Bible so that the full authority
of Scripture is completely undercut.[7]

A church that does not hold to a divinely inspired, authoritative Bible is not a New Testament church; it is an empty shell. Eventually, that organization becomes irrelevant and people do not remain loyal. There are other ways to find an outlet to pursue social action, other places for personal interaction. A believer has no choice but to leave such a church, and certainly a believer searching for a church home cannot come into fellowship with a congregation that does not affirm the inspiration and absolute worth of Scripture.

Why is this belief in the Bible so important? It is important because it is the Bible that was given as a revelation of the being, characteristics, works, and program of God. Second Timothy 3:16–17 tells us,

> All Scripture *is* given by inspiration of God, and *is* profitable for doctrine, for reproof, for correction, for instruction in righteousness, that the man of God may be complete, thoroughly equipped for every good work.

Inspiration was the moving of God by which He communicated His written Word and controlled the writers so that what was written was free from error and was exactly what He wanted to be written. God the Holy Spirit directed

---

[7] Ibid., 44.

human authors to record His intended communication to man. The Spirit moved the authors, used the personalities, circumstances, vocabularies, and experiences of the authors, and employed various literary styles, but the writings that resulted are of divine origin. The Scriptures, both Old Testament and New Testament, are God-breathed, God's words, not man's words; the Scriptures owe their origin to the activity of God. The Holy Spirit who inspired the Word speaks to us today through the Word. One cannot be saved apart from hearing and responding to the truth concerning salvation through Christ that is communicated to us by the Word of God; the message of Scripture is essential to salvation. Conversions come through the explanation of the message of Scripture as one hears, understands, and responds to the Word of God. We are not asked to believe in Jesus as an ancient urban legend; we believe in the Jesus who is carefully communicated to us by the Spirit through the Scriptures. When God brings life, He does it through the Holy Spirit and through His Word. And Scripture is to be our final source for faith and order, indeed for life, after we have responded to the gospel message. "To be thoroughly equipped" means to be completely outfitted, to have everything we need for good works. Why would a church not base everything it attempts to communicate squarely on the Bible?

Solid teaching in a church must include a clear commitment to the teachings of the Bible not only in its statements of belief, but in practice. In Acts 2:42, the early believers "continued steadfastly in the apostles' doctrine and fellowship." In Acts 17:10–12, we learn,

> Then the brethren immediately sent Paul and Silas away by night to Berea. When they arrived, they went into the synagogue of the Jews. These were more fair-minded than those in Thessalonica, in that they received the word with all readiness, and searched the Scriptures daily *to find out* whether these things were so. Therefore many of them believed, and also not a few of the Greeks, prominent women as well as men.

There is a commendation here for the Bereans for their focus on the Scriptures, which brought many of them to faith in Jesus. The Bereans carefully considered the meaning of the Old Testament Scriptures in light of Jesus Christ, and many became believers.

Preaching or teaching in a church based on the New Testament model should be based on accurate interpretation and careful consideration of the true meaning of a passage of Scripture. Sometimes it is difficult to understand Scripture. Professor Lewis Sperry Chafer[8] notes seven basic rules of interpretation for the Bible that are important for us to remember.

---

[8] Lewis Sperry Chafer, revised by John F. Walvoord, *Major Bible Themes*. (Grand Rapids, MI, Zondervan Publishing House, 1976), 33–35.

1. The purpose of the Bible as a whole has to be kept in mind. Each text must be taken in light of the totality of Scripture.
2. The interpretation of Scripture must always take into consideration the purpose of the book of which it is a part.
3. Who is in view in a particular passage must be considered. To whom a particular book or passage is addressed must be determined.
4. The context always must be noted.
5. Similar teachings elsewhere in the Word of God should be compared to the passage under consideration.
6. Accurate exegesis of the words of a particular text is necessary. The words of the original text must be correctly translated and interpreted.
7. Care must be taken not to twist a text in order to make it say something it actually may not say.

When evaluating a church, pay attention to discover if there is consistently the correct interpretation of Scripture in sermons and lessons. Scripture must be the sole authority, Scripture must be held to be of divine origin, Scripture must be held to be infallible and without error, and Scripture must be used correctly.

This is not limited to a doctrinal statement or affirmation of what a church professes to believe. One January I listened to a pastor exhort his small congregation to read their Bibles through during the coming year. Second Timothy 3:16–17 was displayed in his video presentation, and the passage was referred to a couple of times. But the passage was almost reduced to a prop, as he told numerous short stories and personal anecdotes in expressing his opinion that his people should read their Bibles through during the year. He never really explained or used the passage, and he ultimately delivered a lightweight motivational speech designed to interest people in reading the Bible. While the thought was good—reading the Bible is an imperative for every believer—he didn't effectively use the Bible. This pastor would have been far more effective if he had centered his remarks on the passage and then in application presented the challenge to read the Bible. He could have demonstrated a commitment to Scripture and affirmed the value of Scripture in his message. This church has a fine doctrinal statement concerning the Scriptures, but this pastor has missed the vital point of preaching, studying, and proclaiming the Word. In practice, this church does not display a commitment to the Holy Scriptures as the final authority in faith and practice.

A church that does not hold tenaciously to the Bible will often begin to incorporate the surrounding culture, and eventually begin to be deeply influenced by the culture. The message will change. "Sin" will be replaced by "brokenness." Doctrines perceived to be harsh will begin to be ignored and replaced by an emphasis on what meets people's perceived needs and makes people feel better. Eventually, the church will in practice deny the truth of Scripture. Central Christian beliefs will be left behind in a misguided effort to become more relevant and acceptable. While post-modern man has rejected the very idea of objective truth, a church must stand solidly in affirmation of the timeless truth of God as revealed in Scripture.

Church services need to include the careful examination of Scripture. The church is the body of Christ. He is to be at the center of all that happens in a local church body, and we learn of Him through the Bible. The focus of public services cannot be attracting unchurched people, making people feel comfortable, or entertainment. Unchurched people should feel welcome in the public services and invited and encouraged to attend, but the church cannot pander to the culture to gain their attendance. In the book of Acts, people believed the gospel and the church grew rapidly because of preaching from the Scriptures coupled with eyewitness testimony of those who had witnessed the fulfillment of that Scripture in the resurrected Jesus. Unbelievers today need to hear truth from Scripture, not a dumbed-down or overly simplistic message. In fact, preaching should often be profound and challenge the thinking of hearers.

At the heart of the regular gathering of a local church there must be an emphasis on worshiping God through actively hearing, studying, and being challenged from the Word of God. First Timothy 3:15 contains Paul's words: "I write so that you may know how you ought to conduct yourself in the house of God, which is the church of the living God, the pillar and ground of the truth." The church is to read and study the words of Scripture as the basis and ground of its existence. In 2 Timothy 2:15 Paul told Timothy, "Be diligent to present yourself approved to God, a worker who does not need to be ashamed, rightly dividing the word of truth." It is a beautiful thing to see a congregation's people in a church service with open Bibles and notebooks, eagerly hearing an able preacher present a passage of Scripture. The church gathers for worship and equipping, so that believers are then able to minister to each other and to unchurched people. Worship, singing, prayer, and actively listening to the Word demonstrate the attitude of the congregants toward their Christian experience. The preaching of a message from Scripture will have a far more lasting effect on an unchurched individual than will shallow efforts to moralize or entertain. People don't get comfortably entertained into the kingdom of God; they are saved through hearing the Word and responding to the proclaimed grace of God with faith and repentance. The mission of the church toward unbelievers is accomplished first and foremost through the faithful proclamation of the Word. Devotion to the Bible is an absolute essential in the life of a local church.

Without this emphasis on Scripture, a church does not have an effective message or purpose. For attenders to be affected by their attendance, they must have meaningful substance and ideas in the communication they receive; they will not be profited by a church that does not stand strong in the Word and communicate the truth of Scripture.

> We believe in the hot communication of
> content, and as our age cools off more and
> more in its communication, as content is

plowed down and reason is plowed under, I believe the historic Christian faith must more and more consciously emphasize content, content, and then more content.[9]

A church must constantly and intentionally communicate truth from the Bible. As you evaluate a church, ask yourself, "How seriously does this church treat the Bible?" Sermons, music, and prayers all need to be faithful to the Word. There must be content, theology, and challenge in sermons.

The obvious and continual focus of the preacher should be on teaching and preaching the Bible. Pastor and author Mark Dever wrote,

But if you establish the priority of the Word, then you have in place the single most important aspect of the church's life, and growing health is virtually assured, because God has decided to act by his Spirit through his Word.[10]

Look for a church where the Bible is taught and preached.

In the sermon the preacher is not only proclaiming the Word but helping people to hear it through applying it to various needs of the congregation. It has well been said that the duty of the preacher is to so expound the

[9] Schaeffer, 82.
[10] Mark Dever, *Nine Marks of a Healthy Church.* (Wheaton, IL, Crossway, 2013), 43.

Scriptures that in reality the Lord of the church is holding a conversation with His people. In order for this to take place, it goes without saying that the sermon must be an honest attempt to explain the passage of Scripture and not use it for a platform on which to erect the preacher's thoughts or any other human ideas.[11]

Beware of frequent talk of any form of subjective communication from God. God communicates to believers through Scripture. Visions, impressions, dreams, and miraculous signs are not the pattern for the current age. The canon of Scripture is closed. God's communication with believers is through His completed Word. The Spirit certainly leads us, but the Spirit speaks to us first and foremost through the inspired Scriptures. Romans 10:17 reminds us, "So then faith *comes* by hearing, and hearing by the word of God." The Bible is the means through which we have received the Christian faith. Scripture is complete and sufficient to give us an understanding of who God is, who we are, what He has done for us in Christ, and what He expects of us. To deny the Bible is to deny the Christian faith; failure to observe the sufficiency of Scripture as the basis of all a church seeks to communicate betrays the faith as well.

Observe the attitude of the pastor toward the Bible in his presentation; unfortunately, distortions of the message of

---

[11] Saucy, 179.

the Bible are all too common today. This may be motivated by a desire to make difficult teaching easier to accept, a focus on entertaining unchurched people without offending them, or to support misguided ideas. He may simply lack training or ability. There is nothing wrong with using a single verse or even portion of a verse for a sermon text, but it must be done in a manner that makes the teaching consistent with the actual, full meaning of the portion of Scripture within the context of the passage.

Scripture passages are frequently misused to say something they do not actually mean. The King James Version of Proverbs 29:18 begins, "Where there is no vision, the people perish." Sermons have been preached using this phrase to exhort development of a personal vision statement, maintaining a positive attitude to envision and help create a desired end, or to try to create a desire for a corporate vision. The passage does not mean this at all, and to use it in this way is to misuse the text. The verse in the New King James Version reads "Where there is no revelation, the people cast off restraint; But happy is he who keeps the law." This proverb teaches that in the absence of hearing and heeding prophetic vision (i.e., the law, the Scripture), people will go astray, but proclaiming and heeding the Word will bring blessing.

Sadly, this sort of thing is all too common. Acts 6 records the rapid growth of the early church at Jerusalem. The first deacons were appointed to help with meeting the needs of widows and the poor within the congregation while the church leaders concentrated on prayer and study of the Scriptures. I've heard the passage used to demonstrate the value of benevolent acts, implying that the growth of the Jerusalem church mentioned after the appointment of the deacons was the result of benevolent works. The passage doesn't indicate this at all. The church in Acts was growing because of the declaration of the Word and the eyewitness testimony of those who had seen the fulfilment of the Old Testament Scriptures in Jesus. The rapid growth of the church brought into the church many poor people and widows who needed care, but that care was a result, not a cause, of the growing number of believers. The book of Jonah teaches us much more than just finding and surrendering to our perceived personal mission or being affirmed when we encounter difficult circumstances like Jonah did. The book has much important and practical theological teaching, but there is no "me" in Jonah. Easter can be an occasion for misusing Scripture. I once listened to an Easter sermon that was built on the premise that the moved tombstone at the empty grave of Jesus was a metaphor for obstacles we need to have removed in our life. The real point of the moved tombstone, and the point of the empty grave, is much more than a reminder about our personal obstacles; it is that Jesus was alive after being dead, and because of that there is eternal life in Christ. There always needs to be emphasis on the central message of a passage of Scripture, accurate communication of the message of a text, and not imagined or secondary applications.

Preaching and teaching should be solidly biblical, and music a church uses in public worship must also express biblical truth. The congregation should be involved in singing, not just observing entertainment. Congregational singing is powerful as an expression of corporate worship. Melody and harmony should be at the forefront of music used for congregational singing, with percussion in its proper place in the background. Above all, the words that are sung should be substantial, true, and scriptural. There should be a continual focus in the music on God, the Trinity, the grace of God, and the blood, death, burial, and resurrection of Christ for the sins of believers. When music is centered on being trendy and cultural, filled with excitement and emotion, words with a focus on "me" and Jesus primarily as my benefactor, or even when purely secular music is used, beware.

> We should not use music to create the *sense* or *experience* of worshipping God among the unrepentant. They, by definition, cannot worship. Nor should we use music to gain "customers." What do we want in our music? Biblical words or meditations on biblical words. Music that suits the words. Singable and memorable melodies. Instrumentation that allows a congregation to hear themselves sing to one another (Eph. 5:19).[12]

---

[12] Leeman, 76.

Music in a church that is focused on Scripture should not be lifeless, tired, or overly mired in tradition. The days of the little old lady pounding out "Bringing in the Sheaves" on a slightly out-of-tune upright piano are, thankfully, over. The performance quality and scope of music in a local church will be dependent on a variety of factors, such as the size of the congregation. Regardless, a church should feature music that expresses truth in an appropriate, lively, meaningful fashion. The congregation should be involved in singing, and congregational singing should feature music that is designed for congregational singing, not music written for performance or entertainment.

Consider the audiences when a congregation sings. When there is biblical content, music has a teaching purpose, as believers sing truth and doctrine to each other. Unbelievers present in the audience will hear truth, a testimony of the congregation's belief in the message of Scripture. True worship will be offered up to God as the congregation celebrates who He is and what He has done. Hymns can be powerful teaching tools. They can be vehicles to celebrate Scripture and communicate sound doctrine. As a child, I attended a small church that for several years opened the Sunday morning service with the hymn "Holy, Holy, Holy." The words of that song have stuck with me as a bedrock throughout the years. Colossians 3:16 reminds us,

> Let the word of Christ dwell in you richly in all wisdom, teaching and admonishing one another in psalms and hymns and spiritual

songs, singing with grace in your hearts to
the Lord.

Music in a solid church is far more than entertainment or
a warm-up before the sermon; it is corporate worship and
is a celebration of truth.

> Songs of personal experience and aspiration
> can also be worship, but they should not
> take precedence over the proclamation of the
> objective reality of God and the gospel.[13]

We can and should praise God for His daily blessings to
us, but we worship Him when we sing of who He is and
what He has done for us in Christ. "It is therefore of prime
importance that the lyrics of hymns and gospel songs are
expressive of biblical truth."[14]

God strengthens us through singing "psalms, hymns, and
spiritual songs." Through singing, we proclaim words
about God to Him, and He delights when His people gather
before Him and declare truths about Him. He is glorified
in this, and we are edified. From the heart we celebrate the
God who rules and reigns over our life, our triumphs, our
sorrows and weaknesses. Singing by those in a congregation
serves as an encouragement to each other. Ephesians 5:19
tells us to speak to each other in song. When we sing truths
about God's love and faithfulness, those words encourage
other saints who are gathered with us. Nothing empowers

---

[13] Saucy, 185.
[14] Ibid., 186.

us in life more than the Scriptures. When Scripture is proclaimed, God speaks, and so every part of corporate worship services should be filled with the Word. Nothing else is more relevant to the hearts of the people present than the Word of God. It is the Word that gives good news for people. It reminds us that Jesus is the only Savior for lost people, and He is also the Shepherd of His redeemed people.

The attitude of a church toward the Bible is reflected in activities outside of the main weekly worship service. Bible studies and small groups should be more than just general discussion groups and should ultimately convey truth from Scripture. If video presentations are used, they should have biblical content, and discussions of the video need to be kept on topic, not moving into pointless chat. There should be age-appropriate training, such as Sunday school for children. These activities should be conducted by trained, biblically literate individuals, with a focus on presenting Scripture in an interesting manner. Age-appropriate methodology is important to engage the attention of the students. The class or activity cannot be allowed to become boring and must be planned and executed in a way that captures the hearts and minds of the students, but underneath there must be a focus on teaching biblical truth.

As a child, I attended Sunday school every week at a small church. For several years, I had Sunday school quarterlies that were study guides for the weekly Bible lessons. During the week, I filled in the blanks for the coming Sunday's lesson in the quarterly. Later as a junior high-age Sunday school student, the young woman who taught the class encouraged me to read my Bible during the week. She gave me a printed sheet that she had prepared with questions from assigned readings for the week, asked me to turn in my page of questions and answers each Sunday, and provided comments on my answers. I learned the Bible through my experiences at that church.

The purpose and attitude toward youth activities show the commitment of a church toward the Bible. A youth program may present itself as a safe place for kids to "hang out," controlled chaos may be the method of operation, rooms may be decorated with posters of entertainers and movies, the sound of contemporary entertainment music may blare; these should be reason for caution if not alarm. A youth program is a great opportunity for young believers to be challenged to live the Christian life. Teens and young adults want interesting and exciting activities and programs, and the church may have mature, well-grounded individuals to help provide those things, but there can be no substitute for leaders who can faithfully and carefully teach the Word. Adolescents must be convinced by their church that the message of Christianity is vital and real, and they must be challenged to orient their lives around the Bible and its principles for life.

Hebrews 4:12 tells us, "For the word of God is living and powerful, and sharper than any two-edged sword, piercing even to the division of soul and spirit, and of joints and marrow, and is a discerner of the thoughts and intents of the heart." Scripture is the living, active message of God for us. It tells us about the past, present, and future. It shows us the promises God has made and kept through the ages and affirms the promises God has made to us. Look for a church that is committed to sound doctrine and teaching from the Bible. There should be a clear commitment to teaching biblical theology that takes the entire story of the Bible seriously. A preacher you want to listen to must do better than present sermons that twist the text or become nothing more than a Bible-based pep talk. A good church is a Bible-centered church.

CHAPTER 4

Jesus and the Church

He said to them, But who do you say I am?
—Matthew 16:15

Words convey ideas. But often, even with people who seemingly speak the same language, a word will have different meanings. The name *Jesus* is used universally throughout Christendom, but the Jesus of one person is often vastly different than another person's concept of Jesus. The Jesus of the Mormon, the Jesus of the Jehovah's Witness, the Jesus of the non-believer in contemporary society, and the Jesus of the typical evangelical are vastly different. Sadly, the Jesus of many evangelical churches is different than the Jesus of Scripture.

What does the Bible teach about Jesus Christ? Because this is such a vital question, consider it carefully. Scripture tells us that Jesus was the eternal God who came to earth as a human being to live among His people and then to die as the perfect sacrifice to deliver all who repent and believe from the righteous wrath of God. He was both human and divine. His eternality and deity are asserted repeatedly throughout Scripture, which affirms His eternal existence as one with the other persons of the Trinity. The opening section of the gospel of John clearly asserts that He was one with God before creation, and that He became flesh when He was born of a virgin and born in fulfillment of numerous Old Testament prophecies. During His life Jesus worked miracles that demonstrated His deity. His teaching was far different than the teaching of the religious authorities of His day. His teachings and actions captured the attention of people, bringing Him into conflict with the authorities of His society so that they rejected Him and conspired to bring about His death.

Jesus was the only completely sinless individual who ever lived. He was not guilty of any crime, He committed no sin and yet suffered the death of the cross to bear the full cost of human evil. God incarnate humbled Himself to die on our behalf, became the sinless sacrifice to pay the penalty of our sin, and rose from the dead to proclaim the fact that He is Lord of all. He offers eternal life to guilty sinners who come to Him in humble faith and believe in Him as their Savior. The death of Christ secured the salvation of believers and provided the only way for God to forgive human sin while maintaining His holy standard, satisfying the righteous justice of God. Those who come to God through Christ can thus be declared righteous with God, and knowledge of Christ and faith in Him is the only way to righteousness with God. Through the sacrifice of Christ at Calvary, God demonstrated His love for sinners.

Death did not end the life of Jesus. Three days after His death on the cross to atone for the sins of humankind, He rose from the dead. "Jesus Christ and Him crucified" (1 Corinthians 2:2) became the heart of the Christian message, and His resurrection became a central and indispensable truth of the Christian faith. Only when we understand this do we understand who Jesus is and why He was born. The resurrection of Jesus is fundamental to the faith, and no one who denies it can be a true Christian. Without the resurrection of Jesus Christ, there is no salvation, no hope, and no point to the Christian faith.

> The resurrection of Christ because of its historical character constitutes the most important proof for the deity of Jesus Christ. Because it was a great victory over sin and death, it also is the present standard of divine power as stated in Ephesians 1:19–21.[15]

Salvation belongs to those who believe in the atonement, to those who believe in the death, burial, and resurrection of Jesus Christ as historical facts and have by faith acknowledged Him as their only hope of salvation.

Unfortunately, far too many churches do not accept the Bible's teachings about Jesus. To some, He is just a historic figure who left a legacy of great teachings. Many would deny the incarnation, the virgin birth, the deity of Jesus Christ, even while quoting from His teachings. Many

---

[15] Chafer, 68.

39

would deny the resurrection. Some think of His death as that of a martyr who came into conflict with the religious and civil authorities of His society. The idea of the blood atonement, of the necessity of the death and resurrection of Jesus for the sins of others, of God in the flesh as the one plan of God for the salvation of believers, is denied, even considered offensive. But the Bible tells us that sin has affected the whole human race. All who have been born since the garden of Eden have inherited a sin nature; sin is universal. All humans are in a real sense in rebellion against God; the depravity of humankind is total. We don't just live in a "broken" world; we live in the incomprehensible disaster of creatures in rebellion against our Creator. We are sinners without righteousness in need of His righteousness, but through Jesus Christ God has offered us forgiveness, restoration, and salvation.

Attend a church that sets forth this only possible way of salvation from sin and judgement by God's grace through faith in the crucified and risen Lord Jesus Christ. That salvation is not in good works, but by faith in Christ and His death for us. He has reconciled us to God. The centrality of the death of Christ is everywhere in Scripture, not as a martyr or example but a death that satisfied God's holiness.

> Above all else, the Bible is a supernatural book revealing the person and glory of God as manifested in His Son. Such a person as Jesus Christ could never have been the invention of mortal man, for His perfections could never

have been comprehended by the wisest and holiest of this earth. The supreme character of the Bible is supported by its revelation of the supreme character of history in the person of Jesus Christ.[16]

The virgin birth, the atoning death on the cross, and the bodily resurrection from the dead are absolute central truths of the Christian faith, and therefore no church that in any way denies these truths is a church worth attending.

The bodily resurrection of Jesus Christ from the dead is an indispensable element of the faith. In 1 Corinthians 15:14–17, Paul wrote that without the miracle of the resurrection of Christ, faith and the Christian life are futile. Those who say it really doesn't matter if Christ rose from the dead are wrong. Everything in Christianity depends on the resurrection. Christ's being raised from the dead was God's seal on the work Christ accomplished on the cross—the work of our redemption. Leave a church that does not hold to and declare these truths.

Reflecting the writing of theologian J. Gresham Machen in the early twentieth century in defense of the faith, Francis Schaeffer wrote,

> Since liberalism did not believe in fact that Christ died in history to atone for the sins of men and women, and that this was the

---

[16] Ibid., 15

only basis for salvation, liberalism was really religious faith in man dressed up in Christian language and symbols.[17]

A believer simply cannot be a part of a church that does not hold to the virgin birth, the sinless life, and the full deity and humanity of Jesus. A follower of Christ must not be a part of a church that does not believe in the historicity of the resurrection or that does not believe in the necessity of the death, burial, and resurrection of Christ as the only basis for salvation. The church must constantly and loudly proclaim salvation by God's grace through repentance and faith in the Lord Jesus Christ of Scripture. The task for the church is not to seek social justice or build community, create self-esteem, promise success, health, or prosperity, or to use entertainment and marketing techniques to build large organizations. The task of the church is to take the saving knowledge of Jesus Christ to the world.

Many supposed Christians separate Christianity from Christ's central purpose as revealed in Scripture. They might say that the heart of Christianity is simply Jesus's message about God and His love for humanity. But Jesus Christ is more than just a founder who left us an inspiring body of teachings. He is the very heart and soul of Christianity not just in His teachings, but in His redemptive work. A man of unique origin through the virgin birth, He is more than mere man—He is God, and His primary purpose in coming was redemptive. He is the only way to God. In John 14:6

---

[17] Schaeffer, 73.

Jesus says, "I am the way, the truth, and the life. No one comes to the Father except through Me." Acts 4:12 tells us, "Nor is there salvation in any other, for there is no other name under heaven given among men by which we must be saved." One religion is not as good as another, according to Scripture. Universalism, the idea of salvation for all, is not in the Scripture. Salvation is for those who come to God by faith in the atoning work of Jesus Christ.

Are people basically good? Is there merely a need to have the intrinsic goodness within us to be awakened? Surprisingly, even many supposed evangelicals would answer yes to this question. Did the death of Jesus somehow take away the sins of all human beings? If so, a church needs to be a place of moralizing where people are encouraged or have their self-esteem enhanced. But the Bible teaches that atonement is needed because we are in rebellion against the holy God and we need to be reconciled to God. Jesus came as the one by whom we can have a restored relationship with God. I must realize that my fundamental problem is not that I have failed to realize my own potential but that I have sinned against God. Salvation is of divine origin; He has chosen us, and He has regenerated us. We have a responsibility of conversion, responding to God's offer of salvation through faith and repentance. A church needs to present this gospel clearly so individuals can find forgiveness for their sins and find new life in Christ.

We sometimes get the idea that Jesus always attempted to be positive, likable, agreeable, and lovable. A look at His life and ministry shows us that this is not true. He spoke true, cutting words and difficult-to-accept teaching. Truth mattered more to Jesus than did how people reacted to Him. He often stressed points that were completely at odds with the religious teachers of His day. He was not interested in being popular with either the religious authorities or the general populace. While He often spoke of love, He also spoke of difficult and negative subjects. He spoke confrontationally. He spoke of the anger of God against sin. Pastor Matt Chandler wrote,

> Yet I also understand that we can become more concerned with "reaching people" than with being faithful to the Scriptures. And by neglecting the Scriptures, we lose track of what we are reaching people *to*. If it's *to* a God other than the holy, triune creator God of the Bible, or if it's *to* a savior other than the one in the Scriptures who died to appease God's wrath toward sinful people, justifying completely those who repent and believe, then we're no longer offering salvation at all, and we're not building a "church."[18]

The preaching of the gospel of necessity includes presentation of the doctrines of the fall of humankind into sin, justification by faith, imputed righteousness, substitutionary atonement, and Messiah's death as a sacrifice

---

[18] Matt Chandler, foreword, *Word Centered Church*, Jonathan Leeman. (Chicago, IL, Moody, 2017), 12.

to satisfy the righteous wrath of God. In recent years, attacks on those doctrines have come from Protestant and evangelical writers who approach the Bible with the goal of inventing new perspectives on fundamental doctrines, find new interpretations of central biblical passages, or devise a new kind of Christianity. God affirms the vicarious sacrifice of Christ as the only offering that can satisfy His justice and at the same time justify sinners. Only those who know Christ through repentant faith will be declared righteous by God. Knowledge of the Savior is essential. No one gets into heaven without saving knowledge of Him. Thus, the mandate for the church is not to build people's self-esteem, manipulate God so they can become healthy and wealthy, or use marketing gimmicks to grow large churches but rather to spread the saving knowledge of Jesus Christ by proclaiming the gospel. The church cannot become home to a false gospel teaching that is a request that sinners learn to be satisfied with God; the gospel is the announcement that God is satisfied with what Jesus did on behalf of sinners.

This vital belief in Jesus needs to go beyond a point of doctrine or statement of beliefs. The Jesus of Scripture must be at the heart of the church as the church responds to Him as Savior, learns of Him, practices His teachings, anticipates His second coming, and worships Him as Savior and Lord. People need to come to understand the purpose and meaning of the life of Jesus, the purpose of His death, the resurrection of Jesus, and why these things matter. Sermons and lessons about the Jesus of Scripture should be the norm. There needs to be explanation of what sin is and why we need to be saved. The gospel should be presented regularly in sermons and lessons. The great acts of the atonement are the only ground upon which the church can stand, and that needs to be a constant theme.

A primary focus of church music should be words that worship Him, mention the blood, and remember His death, burial, and resurrection. A worshiping congregation should sing of Christ and His substitutionary death on the cross. It is faint praise, or worse, to merely use contemporary entertainment music to sing of Jesus primarily as the source of the good things He does for me in my daily life. Sing of grace, redemption from sin, the satisfying of God's wrath, His promised coming. Sing of His substitutionary death on the cross in our place, which is the heart of the Christian message. The dominant subject of New Testament worship is the manifestation of God's love and grace in redemption through Christ. A church worthy of your membership will not focus on Jesus as merely an additive that can make life better. Joy as well as a sense of reverence and awe characterized the early church, and that attitude should be present in the church you attend. There should be an understanding of the holiness and incomprehensible greatness and majesty of God as well as the fact that He is right here with us. Emotion may be present as a reflection of wonder and praise, but a degree of reverence in worship is a must. In a good church the worship in song will engage the minds and hearts of people in a way that is joyful, dignified without becoming dull, not overly exciting or emotional, but celebrates the truth about Jesus.

Jesus both in His teachings and in His great atoning work should be the center of teaching and preaching in a church. Jesus in His work should be the continual subject of singing. Baptism is identification with Jesus and His death, burial, and resurrection. The ordinance of communion remembers His sacrifice, body, and blood. Prayer should offer praise and thanksgiving for what Jesus has done for us. Everything in a church should be focused on the Lord and Savior.

"What a Friend We Have in Jesus" is a great old gospel song, and He is a friend to His people. But He is not a friend to unbelievers. He is first and foremost God, the second person of the Trinity, who died on the cross and rose again as the only remedy for sin. The gospel is not merely cultivating a relationship or following an example. We must all deal with sin and true guilt, turning from sin and turning to God. Acts 20:21 speaks of "repentance toward God and faith toward our Lord Jesus Christ." We don't just accept Him into our life. We don't invite Him to be our inspiration, our life coach, or our good-luck charm. Before we can think of Jesus as our Friend, before we can call God Father, it is necessary to realize we are a sinner, renounce sin, and turn to Him in faith as our Lord and Savior. We then live for Him, we want to learn of Him and become what He wants us to be, we want to worship Him, and we live in expectation of His return. That will be the message of any church you will want to attend.

CHAPTER 5

The Leadership of the Church

Christians should live moderate, serious, self-restrained lives, and this is especially important for leaders in a church. The New Testament tell us that the church is to be led by men. These men are to be men of ability and of high character, and there should be a plurality of leaders in a local church. First Timothy 2:11–12 tells us, "Let a woman learn in silence with all submission. And I do not permit a woman to teach or to have authority over a man, but to be in silence." A church may have a board or a group of elders who lead, or perhaps a group of deacons, but regardless, the church should have an identified group of leaders who work in conjunction with the lead pastor. Vesting all authority in a single pastor is not wise, and it is not the New Testament pattern. There likely is a lead pastor or teaching pastor who speaks in services and is the perceived leader of the church, but he should lead in concert with others.

These men are not to be new converts but rather mature in their faith and well-respected. They are to be concerned for the spiritual encouragement of others. In the New

Testament letter to Titus, Paul commands Titus to be a model for good works and to teach sound doctrine with sound speech, integrity, and dignity, and he makes the point that younger Christians should be able to look at elders and older members of the faith as an example for a godly life. Christians should have the confidence that if they follow the example of their pastor and church leaders, they will be living a life that is pleasing to God.

The New Testament letters that Paul wrote to Titus and to Timothy lay out the qualities that should be evident in church leaders. In Titus 1:5–10, Paul wrote,

> For this reason I left you in Crete, that you should set in order the things that are lacking, and appoint elders in every city as I commanded you—if a man is blameless, the husband of one wife, having faithful children, not accused of dissipation or insubordination. For a bishop must be blameless, as a steward of God, not self-willed, not quick-tempered, not given to wine, not violent, not greedy for money, but hospitable, a lover of what is good, sober-minded, just, holy, self-controlled, holding fast the faithful word as he has been taught, that he may be able, by sound doctrine, both to exhort and convict those who contradict. For there are many insubordinate, both idle talkers and deceivers.

This passage in Titus gives us several characteristics that are to be present in the life of a church leader. "Blameless" in verse 6 indicates that he is to be above valid ethical criticism and disgrace, possessing the highest character. "Husband of one wife" tells us that he is to be loyal to his wife with no other sexual interest and possessed of moral integrity. No hint of sexual impropriety can be tolerated in church leaders. "Having faithful children, not accused of dissipation or insubordination" means that the faithful church leader should have a well-ordered family life. "Not self-willed," "not quick-tempered," and "not violent" in verse 7 shows us what kind of temperament is to be manifested. Church leadership is not place for a self-absorbed, proud, or overbearing person. A spiritual leader cannot be arrogant, boastful, impatient or easily angered. "Not given to wine" lays out a standard that the Christian leader is to be temperate and not a drinker and not given to excess. A wise church leader will observe a standard of abstinence from alcohol or any other addictive substance. Temperance carries over beyond alcohol, marijuana, and drugs, and there should be no unwholesome addictions or compulsions present in the life of a church leader. "Not greedy for money" describes a person who is not a materialist, not in pursuit of dishonest gain or lacking in financial integrity. Verse 8 speaks of one who is "hospitable," welcoming, and able to interact with other people well and seek their benefit. He should be "a lover of what is good," one who pursues good rather than evil. A "sober minded," "just, holy" man is honorable, respected, mature, and devout; a "self-controlled" person will be a self-disciplined person. He should be mature, both spiritually as well as demonstrating personal maturity, not selfish, obstinate, or childish. Possessed of pure motives, compassion, and concern for people, standing firm for what is right—these are qualities of a church leader.

Titus 2:2 says "that the older men be sober, reverent, temperate, sound in faith, in love, in patience." These men are to be in control of themselves, not characterized by following unhealthy desires, impulses, and passions. They are to be free of harmful addictions. They are to be stable, steadfast, worthy of respect, and growing in their likeness to Christ. These men are to be dignified, not frivolous, sound and solid in their faith, showing the highest integrity, uncorrupt, serious, and sound in speech. In Titus 2:6–8, speaking to "younger men," Paul reminds that they are to be "sober-minded, in all things showing yourself to be a pattern of good works, in doctrine showing integrity, reverence, incorruptibility, sound speech that cannot be condemned, that one who is an opponent may be ashamed, having nothing evil to say of you."

These repeated themes in the book of Titus are to be the marks of a church leader.

Paul told Timothy these same things. In 1 Timothy 3, Timothy is reminded of the need for personal integrity.

> This *is* a faithful saying: If a man desires the position of a bishop, he desires a good work. A bishop then must be blameless, the husband of one wife, temperate, sober-minded, of good

behavior, hospitable, able to teach; not given to wine, not violent, not greedy for money, but gentle, not quarrelsome, not covetous; one who rules his own house well, having *his* children in submission with all reverence (for if a man does not know how to rule his own house, how will he take care of the church of God?); not a novice, lest being puffed up with pride he fall into the *same* condemnation as the devil. Moreover he must have a good testimony among those who are outside, lest he fall into reproach and the snare of the devil. (1 Timothy 3:1–7)

He is to be mature in the faith as well as in his personal life and character. As to the instruction concerning a novice, Robert Saucy wrote,

> The Greek word means literally "newly planted" and refers to the fact that that the office of the overseer is not for the new convert but demands spiritual maturation. The concept of thrusting a believer into such a position in order to encourage his maturing is prohibited.[19]

Mature, not a novice, able to react positively to difficulty, responding with love to people and concerned about

---

[19] Saucy, 148.

others, content, sober-minded, and secure—these are to characterize a worthy church leader.

The church leader should be considerate, welcoming, and gentle toward others, careful about anger, not violent, cautious and not quick to quarrel, resistant to temptations from whatever source. He should be able to communicate God's truth effectively, with a well-ordered life that confirms that communication. "Let the elders who rule well be counted worthy of double honor, especially those who labor in the word and doctrine." Patterns of life and of conduct that make them worthy to be honored—those are the kind of people to lead a church.

> Leadership in the church should be invested in those who seem to evidence in their own lives, and who are able to promote in the life of the congregation as a whole, the edifying and sanctifying work of the Holy Spirit.[20]

First Timothy 5:17 implies that those who give direction should be good managers. A church needs to be effectively organized, and its business affairs need to be conducted in a professional and organized manner by people of high ethical standards. Poor or dishonest business dealings can have a profoundly negative effect on a church.

How Christians display their faith is a matter of great importance, as what we believe and how we behave has

[20] Dever, 35.

an impact on the people we influence. This is particularly the case with identified leaders, and therefore the Bible sets high standards. The church should be led by men who are responsible, self-controlled, wise, and refrain from overindulgence. Men who act appropriately to the situation. Men who have a servant's heart, who are kind and generous. Men who lead their families well. Committed believers who are serious about matters of sin, serious about the reaching the lost, serious about eternal matters, manifesting grace. Men who have the maturity to get out of their T-shirt and jeans and dress with dignity when it is appropriate. Men who younger men both in age and in the faith can follow and learn from.

While these general qualities are to be present in the totality of leadership, they should be especially present in the lead pastor. Character, reputation, ability to handle the Word, and demonstration of the fruit of the Spirit enable the pastor as shepherd to lead, guard, protect, and feed the congregation. He is responsible to teach God's Word, to communicate God's truth faithfully. Second Timothy 4:2 contains the command to "preach the word," which is the prime directive for the pastor. Titus 1:9 tells us "holding fast the faithful word as he has been taught, that he may be able, by sound doctrine, both to exhort and convict those who contradict." He is to "hold firmly"; there is to be no wavering in his convictions about Scripture, no deviations from the total message. In a real sense, the pastor must be a theologian. His teaching is to encourage the church, and he is to refute those who oppose the truth of Scripture. The pastor is to speak what is both true and substantive. First Timothy 3:2 reminds us, "A bishop then must be blameless, the husband of one wife, temperate, sober-minded, of good behavior, hospitable, able to teach"—confident, principled, of high character, and able to communicate God's truth, mature in sound doctrine. The life of the teacher of the Word has to be consistent with his words, and the preaching of the Word must be absolutely central to his ministry to the church.

The pastor's sermons need to be clearly in line with what the Bible teaches. Second Timothy 2:15–16 reminds us,

> Be diligent to present yourself approved to God, a worker who does not need to be ashamed, rightly dividing the word of truth. But shun profane *and* idle babblings, for they will increase to more ungodliness.

In Titus 1:10–11, warning against false teachers, Paul wrote,

> For there are many insubordinate, both idle talkers and deceivers, especially those of the circumcision, whose mouths must be stopped, who subvert whole households, teaching things which they ought not, for the sake of dishonest gain.

Note the characteristics here of the false teachers who are to be opposed. They are rebellious and unruly—in opposition to accepted Christian principle. They speak words that have little real substance and say nothing of significance in comparison with Scripture. The false teachers do not clearly teach Scripture, while a faithful pastor uses the Scriptures as the foundation and substance of his ministry.

Determining a sermon's value and faithfulness to Scripture sometimes takes careful analysis and discernment. Reading a passage at the beginning or referencing a couple of verses during the sermon does not guarantee that the sermon is faithful to the message of the Bible. Read the extended context of the Scripture passages, determine their meaning, and compare that with the message of the speaker. Context is always the most important factor in understanding a shorter passage. Is he using a passage out of context to merely reinforce his opinions? Is the emphasis a secondary application of the passage that is not in fact the main point of the passage? There needs to be faithfulness to the Scripture, not a new or novel idea that is not clearly in the Bible. Preaching needs to be completely faithful to the message of Scripture, but it also needs to be more than academic. Good preaching takes Scripture and passionately conveys truth and applies it to the hearers. It seeks to inform people but also to move them to action or decision.

A preacher teaches and leads through the ministry of the Word, not motivational speeches, book reviews, calls to social action, or telling entertaining anecdotes or stories. Most good preachers use appropriate illustrations in their preaching, but the basis and substance of their sermon needs to be from Scripture. The pastor is not to divert from the task of declaring the Word. Whatever his other failings or abilities, he must have the demonstrated ability to preach the Word.

Mark Dever has written, "If you are looking for a good church, the role of the preacher of God's Word is the most important thing to consider."[21] Further, he writes,

> Be very careful before joining a church that does not stress expositional preaching, or calling a preacher who is not an expositional preacher, who is not committed to preaching all of God's Word, regardless of how uncomfortable parts of it may make us feel.[22]

An expositional preacher explains a passage of Scripture based on careful, diligent study of a passage; he leads his congregation in carefully considering Scripture that he has diligently studied. He preaches and applies Scripture after explaining and interpreting his text, being careful to remain faithful to the true original meaning of the passage in its context and in the context of the totality of the Bible.

Expository preaching is completely faithful to the original teaching of a passage and then moves from what a passage meant for the original recipients to an application of why it is important for its hearers today. Preaching of the Word takes place when the truth of a passage of Scripture is proclaimed and brought to bear on life. A good sermon will

---

[21] Ibid., 58.
[22] Ibid., 217.

have a clear theme or central thought, and that central idea needs to be from Scripture and in line with the teaching of the particular passage under consideration. God uses the proclaimed Word to give life, and through the Scripture, God changes lives. He continues to nourish His people through it as they are admonished, corrected, and trained. Unbelievers come to faith and believers grow in their faith through actively hearing, understanding, and believing the gospel.

Increasingly, preaching in evangelical churches has diverted away from Scripture. In circles where the inspiration and authority of the Bible are not held as true, this is bound to be the case. Sadly, this is even the case among supposed evangelicals who give lip service to a belief in Scripture. Nice sentiments loosely based on the Sermon on the Mount will perhaps be presented, but not detailed proclamation of Scripture. Jesus might be spoken of as a friend or an inspiration, but not as God, Savior, the one atoning sacrifice for sin. There may be calls to benevolence or social action. The pastor might be entertaining, a great story teller, a great motivational speaker, but if he does not preach the Word, he is an imposter.

The proclaimed message must be faithful to the entire theme and body of Scripture. The central theme of Scripture is the death, burial, and resurrection of Jesus Christ as the substitutionary sacrifice for sin. The gospel has transformational effects on individuals and by extension on society, but the theme of Scripture does not center on making people feel happy or comfortable in this life. A preacher and church that seemingly are focused on fitting into culture and affirming people to make them happier, wealthier, more successful, and fulfilled individuals is not being true to the message of Scripture. When considering the preaching ministry of a church, determine if the promises and affirmations of Scripture are taken out of context and misapplied. Are the New Testament affirmations to believers applied in a general sense without noting that they are for believers? Jesus didn't come primarily to be an example, teacher, inspiration, or friend; He came to reveal the Father and to be the one true and only sacrifice for sin. That should be the clear teaching of the church and of its pastor.

Spiritual growth of people will be the result of the consistent preaching of Scripture. We see this principle in Paul's letters. We've already noted it in Titus and the Timothy epistles. In Ephesians 4:11–13 he wrote,

> And He Himself gave some *to be* apostles, some prophets, some evangelists, and some pastors and teachers, for the equipping of the saints for the work of ministry, for the edifying of the body of Christ, till we all come to the unity of the faith and of the knowledge of the Son of God, to a perfect man, to the measure of the stature of the fullness of Christ.

Pastor and theologian John MacArthur wrote, "The call to the ministry is not a call to a profession; it's a passion. God gives gifted men to the church, not to entertain it, program it, or organize it, but to bring believers to maturity."[23]

All believers, not just pastors, are responsible to communicate the gospel to others, and this happens in a variety of ways. Proclaiming the message of the Bible can happen in an informal conversation or in a formal counseling session. Parents teach the Word to their children around the dinner table and in the normal activities of daily life. An opening to proclaim the Word can come through the sending of a get-well card to a sick friend, by various acts of kindness, or in a telephone conversation. The Word can be presented by men, women, and children of every age and station in life. All of us are responsible to communicate God's Word to others. Part of the way we develop the ability to effectively "preach the Word" in our own everyday lives is to be equipped to do so by the teaching and preaching we hear at church. Those who teach in a church, whether the lead pastor, Sunday school teachers, or small group leaders, need to be "able to teach." They need to be able to direct sermons, lessons, or discussions toward the substance of the Scriptures. As you evaluate a church, consider how well that church prepares its members to be communicators of the gospel message.

---

[23] John MacArthur Jr., *The Church the Body of Christ*. (Grand Rapids, MI, Zondervan, 1973), 118.

The New Testament repeatedly warns against false teachers and unworthy leaders in the church. Acts 20:29 warns against false teachers as "savage wolves." First Timothy 6:3–5 warns,

> If anyone teaches otherwise and does not consent to wholesome words, *even* the words of our Lord Jesus Christ, and to the doctrine which accords with godliness, he is proud, knowing nothing, but is obsessed with disputes and arguments over words, from which come envy, strife, reviling, evil suspicions, useless wranglings of men of corrupt minds and destitute of the truth, who suppose that godliness is a *means of* gain. From such withdraw yourself.

Second Peter 2:1 warns against "false teachers among you." Jude 4 mentions "unfaithful teachers who have crept in unnoticed." Often, these false teachers are not easy to immediately identify. It will take keen discernment.

Before you attempt to evaluate a local church, read Titus and 1 and 2 Timothy. Then, read them again. If the pastor doesn't measure up to the standards enumerated in these letters of Paul, that church is not a church you want to attend.

CHAPTER 6

The Christian Life and the Church

The Christian life begins when we respond to the gospel with repentant faith and a willingness to follow Jesus. The longer we follow Him, the more we are to leave our old self behind. We "put off the old man with his deeds" and "put on the new man with his deeds" (Colossians 3:9–10). We "put on the new man which was created according to God, in true righteousness and holiness" (Ephesians 4:24). The church constantly remembers what Christ has done for us in the past and often speaks of the future promised to us by faith. The church also must prepare us to live in the present. Francis Schaefer wrote,

> Evangelism is primary, but it is not the end of our work and indeed cannot be separated from the rest of the Christian life. We must acknowledge and then act upon the fact that

> if Christ is our Savior, he is also our Lord in
> *all* of life.[24]

There are perhaps three general ways that a church might approach Christian living, and the approach to the Christian life in a church is usually easy to detect. One approach would be to center on man-made rules, a sort of Pharisaical legalism. Church members are expected to order their lives and conduct around rules espoused by the church. The underlying thought is that we somehow need to gain favor with God through observing man-made rules. The mentality is "Don't smoke, don't chew, and don't associate with those who do." There may be a perceived dress code and rigid standards, lifestyle rules, and appearance standards are mentioned often in church, and there may be a focus on minutiae and nonessentials. While some congregants might accept this thinking, it will often be rejected and cause harm and offense.

If a member of this first kind of church is discovered in a restaurant with an alcoholic drink, they are at risk of being frowned upon, judged, or shunned. A second approach is to simply reject standards. A member of such a congregation might be invited to have a drink with a church leader. In this antinomian or rule-free approach, tradition and piety are ignored, and established conventions and ideas of life and conduct are dismissed or even ridiculed. People are led to believe that they can for the most part do anything they want. Church leaders attend services dressed casually,

---

[24] Schaeffer, 39.

and congregants dress as casually and conveniently as they choose. Standards for conduct in daily life are seldom mentioned, as the church attempts to "put the fun back into religion." People are left with the feeling that they are for the most part free to act and present themselves any way they choose. Fitting into current culture is a priority and is preferred to standing at all apart from society. Lifestyle advice might center on relational issues but not personal holiness or piety.

This church won't talk about sin, instead focusing on felt needs and assuaging guilt not in a sinful world, but in a "broken world" or "imperfect world." It also won't talk much about eternal life but will talk much about improving life now. There may be a focus on community, social justice issues, personal relationships, material gain, and success in life, but not much focus on the eternal life promised in Scripture to those who give themselves to the Lord. Congregants are learning mere human wisdom, rather than divine wisdom, with Christian terminology woven in. This brings an inadequate understanding of sin, repentance, and purpose in the Christian life. The pastor may assure his hearers that "We've all failed and made mistakes but don't worry because God loves you." "As long as you're doing your best and desire to do what's right, you can be assured God is pleased with you." "When your inner voice reminds you have made a mistake, you should say, 'That's okay. God loves me.'" In essence, sin is no big deal. The communication is that life is not so much meant to bring glory to God but is meant to bring happiness and ease to the individual.

The Bible teaches us something different from either of these errors.

> Next to the way of salvation, there is no more important theme to be mastered by the human mind than the divine plan whereby a Christian may live to the glory of God.[25]

When a person responds to the gospel, his or her life is to be radically changed. Sanctification is the process that begins at salvation and causes us to become what Christ would have us to be. The believer is "in Christ, he is a new creation" (2 Corinthians 5:17). Paul wrote in Romans 12:1–2,

> I beseech you therefore, brethren, by the mercies of God, that you present your bodies a living sacrifice, holy, acceptable to God, which is your reasonable service, And do not be conformed to this world, but be transformed by the renewing of your mind, that you may prove what is that good and acceptable and perfect will of God.

We become a student of Christ and His Word. We develop a new worldview, and our lifestyle is completely affected. We alter our lifestyle and conduct not because of rules

---

[25] Chafer, 190.

and regulations but because we respond to Christ and His Word.

While we never become completely sinless, our goal becomes to sin less. Sin is never okay; we can never excuse sin and can never minimize it. At the same time, 1 John 1:9 tells us, "If we confess our sins, He is faithful and just to forgive us our sins and to cleanse us from all unrighteousness." The church speaks out against sin and confronts sin, but the end in view is not condemnation but rather confession, repentance, restoration, and forgiveness.

In a legalistic atmosphere, a person might be taught that they must act and dress in a certain proscribed manner. But without a biblical basis for life, they ultimately may reject that teaching. When they are caught in a failure, they may be rejected or judged. The antinomian church doesn't give a person a solid foundation for life, but assures them that, for the most part, whatever they do is okay. When their conduct causes failure or difficulty, the antinomian church assures people that it isn't a problem, and they should pick themselves up, start over again, and not feel bad. A biblical church will neither judge people who do not follow man-made rules nor affirm people in their sins and just encourage them to feel inspired and be the best person they can be. A biblical church will teach and challenge people to repent of sin and respond in faith to the gospel, and then challenge believers to be the person God wants them to be, to live like a servant of their Lord and Savior Jesus Christ.

The task of the church is not merely to make people feel better in a man-centered approach. The task of the church is to help people move away from a concentration on their perceived needs and desires and realize true spiritual issues in light of eternity. In 1 Corinthians 6, Paul shows he no longer thinks like the Jewish legalist he had been. He urges his readers to not just observe rules but to enjoy a new way of living in the Spirit and love of Christ. He pointedly urges his readers to flee from immorality and sin. He reminds them of the truth that they belong to the one who bought them with His blood, and that therefore they are to honor Him. The direction of the church should be to focus on the Lord of the Church and teach people to worship God in the totality of life. Our goal and purpose in life is to become like Jesus in attitude, character, and conduct. The church presents the Bible to us so we might be instructed and challenged to live in submission to Christ.

> Although the sanctification of the church is complete and perfect in its positional standing in Christ, it is also a process in the life of the church as the meaning and significance of that complete salvation are continually applied through the operation of the Holy Spirit by means of the Word.[26]

The New Testament refers to believers as "bondservants" in Titus 1:1, James 1:1, 2 Peter 1:1, and Jude 1. The word translated *bondservant* is a word that, basically, means slave.

---

[26] Saucy, 96.

Believers are to think of themselves in a very real sense as a slave of Jesus. Titus 1:1 speaks of "acknowledgement of the truth which accords with godliness," and this letter of Paul reminds us to live in view of what Christ has done for us. The apostle reminded Titus to teach people what is to be expected of people who have been redeemed by God's grace. Avoid the sinful pressures of the world, live an orderly, self-controlled life, remain morally upright, live a godly life—these are to be the patterns of life for believers. The task of a church is to move believers to live as "slaves" of Jesus Christ.

The Puritan writer Thomas Manton wrote,

> If we could make ourselves, then we could live for ourselves. If we could be our own first cause, then we might be our own end. But God made us for himself, and sent us into the world for himself. It is not our duty to glorify God in heaven only, but also here on earth in the midst of difficulties and temptations.[27]

Attend a church that stands in clear witness, confrontation, and antithesis to the surrounding culture, not a church that is transfixed with accommodation of contemporary ideas.

The church has a commission to move their congregations toward living lives characterized by humility, purity, godliness, separation from sinful practices, sacrifice, and

---

[27] Thomas Manton, *Works of Thomas Manton*, Volume 1. Edinburgh, Banner of Truth, 1993, 81.

faithfulness. Sanctification is a work of the Holy Spirit, and pastors are charged with the task of seeing the image of Christ developed in the lives of their congregants. By hearing and responding to the teaching of the Word, people will become what God would have them to be, and then they will be able to affect their world. A worthy pastor will be devoted to the spiritual growth of his people. Avoid the church leader focused more on being relevant, entertaining, cool, contemporary, inclusive, social, or innovative than he is on moving people toward being like Christ.

Believers need to be maturing in their faith, growing, becoming stronger. "The Christian life is the process of working out in practical matters the spiritual resources of the believer's position in Christ."[28] Second Peter 3:18 tells us to "grow in the grace and knowledge of our Lord and Savior Jesus Christ." That is why a strong relationship with the Word is so important. Mark Dever wrote, "The Word of God must be central to our lives as individuals and as a church because God's Spirit uses the Word to create faith in us and to make us grow."[29] Focus on Scripture is more than just an academic learning of facts. Knowledge of God's truth translates into spiritual growth and maturity that enables people to live the life that God intends for His people. John MacArthur wrote, "The Word of God taught by men of God brings growth in the people of God."[30]

---

[28] MacArthur, 20.
[29] Dever, 57.
[30] MacArthur, 119.

Just as the local church is the primary means of evangelism, so the local church is a primary means of helping believers to grow in their faith. As we are instructed by the Bible and hear it proclaimed, it will change our lives and enable us to become strong, mature believers. The importance of attending a church where to Word is faithfully taught and preached cannot be overemphasized. It is a key to living the Christian life. Our life is affected by what we know of Scripture. A church should remind us often of what Christ has done for us. A church should help us focus on the fact that Jesus is coming again and that Christianity is very much eschatological, focused on our eternal destiny beyond this life. But the church also equips us to live as believers in the present.

CHAPTER 7

Other Considerations

Previously, I have discussed some areas that are non-negotiables. A worthy church will hold tenaciously to the authority and sufficiency of Scripture and the essential doctrines taught in Scripture, especially to the biblical teachings concerning Jesus. A church in the New Testament pattern will be led by men of high character and substance who are ministering to the congregation in a manner that will help the people to grow in their faith. There are other considerations that are important, including some that are not absolute. Aspects of churches will vary, for instance, based on the community where they are located. A church meeting in a dense urban area is likely to look quite different than a church in a small town or suburban setting, and a new church without a permanent place of meeting may have different characteristics than an established church. The economic and ethnic makeup of the surrounding community will naturally influence the characteristics of a church.

The distance from your home to the place a church meets should be considered. A long commute will make it more difficult for you to attend regularly and might isolate you from regular contact and fellowship with others in the church. When you plan to relocate your place of residence, it might be wise to find a church home in the general area first and then locate nearby.

The general atmosphere of a church, the "vibe" if you will, is important. This can be manifested in many ways. How are you greeted and made to feel on your first and subsequent visits? Does the church have an inordinate number of "odd" people? The body of Christ is composed of people of all races, ages, economic statuses, levels of intelligence, and abilities, but the local church should be made up primarily of "normal," mainstream people. You will want to be in a church where you can enjoy fellowship with people with whom you can identify. Ideally a church will include people of a variety of age groups, and not be generationally focused to the exclusion of others. A church should be composed of a fair representation of the surrounding community. A multiethnic church is a good thing.

Is there an atmosphere of love and acceptance? Christians are to love one another; that is a hallmark of the church. First Thessalonians 3:12 tells us, "And may the Lord make you increase and abound in love to one another and to all, just as we *do* to you." Jesus said, recorded in John 13:34–35,

A new commandment I give to you, that you
love one another; as I have loved you, that you
also love one another. By this all will know
that you are my disciples, if you have love for
one another.

Believers should enjoy being together with other believers.
You should be able to detect that commitment. How are
visitors treated who may not fit in with the congregation?
Love, acceptance, and forgiveness are to be at the basis of
relationships among believers, and that should be manifested
toward people who are not part of the congregation as well.
The church never accommodates, endorses, or excuses sin,
but the church must manifest the love of Christ.

Consider the atmosphere of the service. Is the service
cold and lifeless, the music uninspired and ritualistic, the
sermon purely academic? Is it overly formal? Or is it overly
informal? Do the pastor and others involved in the service
show an attitude of respect for the Lord and the gathering of
His body? How are the leaders and congregants dressed? Do
the people come dressed in their pajamas and flipflops, or
do they come dressed in a manner reflecting respect toward
the body of Christ and maturity as Christians representing
their Savior, the Lord of the church? Is the service loud and
raucous, with no sense of reverence, designed to reflect
the entertainment style of current culture, with the pastor
seeking to entertain, coach, or motivate without a clear
examination of the Word of God? Is the atmosphere that
of a youth camp or a Christian version of a nightclub or the

corner bar? Before you commit to a church, you will want it to feel like church, not overly tied to tradition, not focused on being trendy.

Fun and entertaining should not be the first words that come to mind when you think of a church. Don't just ask children after attending if they had fun. Ask them to tell you what they learned. Ask yourself what you learned, what lasting value did your experience hold. Being warm and engaging is important in the communication process, but there is no substitute for communication with truth and content and application of biblical truth that has lasting value. Fun and fellowship are no replacement for impact.

If a church is extremely small, there may be valid reasons why the church is small. The church may be a recent church plant or may be working to overcome problems that have led to its decline. On the other hand, a drop in attendance or lack of growth may indicate ongoing problems that you will need to discover and consider before committing to the church. A small church won't have particularly robust programs but may offer opportunities for a new member to get involved and make a difference. You may simply be more comfortable in a healthy, small church. On the other hand, you may find it easier to visit a larger church, as you will be less likely to be singled out as a visitor. A larger church will offer more activities. One danger of a large church is that it will become easy for you to continue to attend anonymously without ever getting actively involved. In a very large church, you may never get to have any involvement with the teaching pastor; this lack of personal contact can be mitigated by becoming involved with people in a small group or class.

Be cautious about a multilocation megachurch. Churches birthing other churches is a good thing, and sometimes a growing church may have services at a satellite location before spinning off that location as an independent church. But churches where services become an experience akin to going to a movie are not a good pattern. You are unlikely to find solid Bible teaching and preaching in this kind of church. Preachers should be more than entertainers or movie stars on a screen. The last thing we need in this century is more impersonal screen time. There is no substitute for being able to interact with and be in the presence of the minister.

Churches in the Western world, particularly in the United States, have the blessing of owning properties to use as houses of worship. The heart of a local church can often be seen in its place of meeting. Especially when evaluating a smaller congregation, the state of repair of a facility can be an important consideration. When a church does not have a well-maintained, attractive building, it is a poor statement to the community; it also indicates that the congregation may not hold their church with enough esteem to invest time, effort, and money into their facility. The heart, and treasure, of the people is not there. A small congregation, particularly in a smaller community, may not have the resources to build an elaborate facility or may not chose to invest in an ornate building, but that is not an excuse to neglect proper maintenance of the building that the church does have. When there is respect for the congregation and the activities that happen at the church facility, it demands that the building be maintained properly. There should be anticipation and planning for basic repair and maintenance, including janitorial service, landscaping, and snow removal. A local church that does not show a desire or ability to do this may have underlying problems that need to be corrected.

Particularly with larger congregations and newer facilities, the facility tends to reflect the intention and attitude of the leadership toward what is to happen at the church. The room where the congregation meets for its regular services should reflect the fact that the congregation meets to joyfully and respectfully worship and to hear and consider the preaching and teaching of the Word of God. It should quite simply look and feel like a place for contemplation, prayer, and instruction, where people reflect on a transcendent God of immense grandeur and glory. If a facility mimics a contemporary entertainment venue, then likely it *is* at least to some degree merely an entertainment venue.

The absence or presence of a pulpit can be telling. A pulpit certainly does not guarantee that the message of the speaker is substantial or true. Bad things have been declared from behind pulpits for as long as churches have had buildings. But do not ignore the fact that entertainers or motivational speakers do not use pulpits, and if a pastor does not have a pulpit, he may be in the trap of being an entertainer or motivational speaker instead of a faithful preacher of the Word of God. A pulpit as a focal point in front of the congregation encourages and implies an attitude of focus on the Bible. Churches historically have had pulpits front and center stage to symbolize the centrality of the Word and to facilitate the speaker's use of his Bible and his notes. A careful, faithful preacher dedicated to teaching and preaching the Word will likely have prepared notes to help maintain focus on his message. A speaker not focused on Scripture may have a small lectern to hold his water bottle and computer or Bible, but feels free to physically wander around the stage and likely will wander around in his speech as well. He becomes the focus, not the Scripture.

Accommodation to current culture is something to be avoided. Three decades ago Francis Schaefer warned,

> And let us understand that to accommodate to the world spirit about us in our age is nothing less than the most gross form of worldliness in the proper definition of that word. And with this proper definition of worldliness, we must say with tears that, with exceptions, the evangelical church is worldly and not faithful to the living Christ.[31]

He went on to write of those who would accommodate culture,

---

[31] Schaefer, 38.

What they are saying is this: "We are the 'new evangelicals,' the 'open evangelicals': we have thrown off the cultural isolation and anti-intellectualism of the old fundamentalists." But what they have not noticed is that they have nothing to say which stands in clear confrontation and antithesis to the surrounding culture.[32]

More recently, Mark Dever wrote,

Simply put, we need churches that are self-consciously distinct from the culture. We need churches in which the key indicator of success is not evident results but persevering biblical faithfulness.[33]

You will want to be part of a church that is in large measure countercultural. Belief in absolute truth has been rejected by postmodern society, but the Bible is absolute; God doesn't adjust His thoughts based on man's current ideas. Among many in the evangelical community, Jesus has been seemingly reduced to a friend, an inspiration, a coach, or a good luck charm. Be part of a church that proclaims Him as God, as Savior, as the Atoning Sacrifice, as the one plan of God for man's salvation. Christianity has powerful transforming results in the present lives of believers, but Jesus didn't come primarily to make us happy, healthy,

---

[32] Ibid., 99.
[33] Dever, 32.

prosperous, successful, or fulfilled. He came to save us from sin, to give us eternal life, to bring honor and glory to God. Don't be a part of a church that overtly attempts to be "trendy," to merely meet the perceived needs of prosperous postmodern narcissists, to entertain in a culturally acceptable manner in a misguided attempt to reach people. Be a part of a church that with wonder, reverence, and a sense of awe worships and serves the One True and Living God as revealed in His Word. That is countercultural, and that is exactly what is necessary.

CHAPTER 8

Make the Commitment

Christians are not to be detached from other followers of Christ, and believers should strive to be in the mainstream of a solid local church. A characteristic of the believer in the New Testament is love for other believers, living in unity for the sake of the gospel. Followers of Christ need each other. Believers need to be discipled and to be instructed from the Bible. Every follower of Christ needs to be involved in service, to stay sensitive to opportunities for service, and most often that happens within a local congregation. Consumerism, seeing church completely as a spectator sport, has grown among Christians in recent decades. When we're not satisfied, we can just find another church where we can be a consumer. But we need to be more than consumers, critics, or spectators; we need to be actively involved in service.

Reaching lost people should always be a focus of believers, and the church exists to proclaim the gospel. The church should be involved in equipping members to do the work of the ministry, enabling believers to be a witness to the people in their lives, teaching the Word so people gain the ability to present the gospel in clear, biblical terms. Paul wrote to the Ephesians that the gifted teachers of the church were given "for the equipping of the saints for the work of the ministry, for the edifying of the body of Christ" (Ephesians 4:12). An evangelistic focus is necessary, vital, and at the very heart of the purpose for the existence of a church. The New Testament pattern is that the church does that primarily by a focus on believers growing in their faith so that believers grounded in the faith and excited about their relationship with Christ and His church are able to reach the people around them with the gospel.

A church should welcome unbelievers into their public services, open and genuinely welcoming to any and all. Congregants should be challenged to bring people to church in order that they might hear the gospel and experience the presence of worshipping believers. While sermons must over time focus on a variety of texts and topics from Scripture, unbelievers should hear relevant material from Scripture that will help them come to terms with their need for Christ.

The emphasis on reaching the unchurched, however, should not translate into focusing public services on the unchurched. The American church in recent years has been infected with the thought that in order to reach people we need to modify the message and focus of the church. That idea has produced supposed churches that are massive in size, and this concept has permeated the American church from the largest to the smallest. Motivational talks have replaced biblical sermons. Content has been lost; preaching of Scripture has been pushed to the background and even ridiculed by some. Declaring the hard truths of Scripture has been neglected and replaced with a mentality of, "God loves you and accepts you just as you are." Personal success, felt needs, prosperity, relational healing, and social issues have become the focus with this mentality. Music of majesty and truth has been lost, replaced by loud percussion-driven, contemporary-sounding pop tunes with low-content words of faint praise focused often on individual experience. Corporate worship has been lost. Find out what people want, make them comfortable, and attract them to events has become the dominant thought. Subjects like sin, repentance, and faith make people uncomfortable, so they are avoided. Increasingly, the doctrine of original sin and the sin nature have been forgotten. Grace has been redefined to a concept that says God really likes you and accepts you just as you are, so you should just pick yourself up, dust yourself off, and start over again when you fail or feel bad. Such an approach, however, is not a fulfillment of the commission to the church to reach the lost. It is a deception that helps people feel more comfortable as they travel down the broad road that leads to destruction.

As you consider becoming part of a church, ask some questions. Will you be excited to invite people to attend this church with you? Is the church Christ-centered and gospel focused, with an obvious focus on the Bible, or is the church entertainment focused, with shallow sermons featuring a few verses thrown in for effect? Do they preach the gospel, and do they correctly handle the Word? Does the emphasis seem to be on felt needs, self-help, and success in life, or is there an emphasis on Scripture, the gospel, sin and grace, heaven and hell? Is Scripture recognized as sufficient, as the complete revelation of God, or is there an unhealthy emphasis on subjective extrabiblical communication? Do the pastor and teachers teach the Bible, or do they tell stories and speak of other things as they throw in a few out-of-context verses or phrases? Is the music sound, featuring a variety of Christian hymns and gospel songs that teach biblical doctrine, or merely easy entertainment-focused songs with little real content? Does the church help Christians understand the Bible and challenge them to grow in their faith? The church should cause you to think, question, and gain wisdom and spiritual maturity. Does the church focus both on the present Christian life and eternity in light of what Christ has done for us? Does the church mention the second coming of Christ and project an attitude of anticipating the coming of Christ? Are the pastor and leaders open, approachable, and forthright? The pastor should not be an autocrat but should be available and willing to answer questions and discuss issues.

Hebrews 10:19–25 reminds us,

> Therefore, brethren, having boldness to enter the Holiest by the blood of Jesus, by a new and living way which He consecrated for us, through the veil, that is, His flesh, and *having*

a High Priest over the house of God, let us draw near with a true heart in full assurance of faith, having our hearts sprinkled from an evil conscience and our bodies washed with pure water. Let us hold fast the confession of *our* hope without wavering, for He who promised *is* faithful. And let us consider one another in order to stir up love and good works, not forsaking the assembling of ourselves together, as *is* the manner of some, but exhorting *one another,* and so much the more as you see the Day approaching.

We are part of a church to contribute to the spiritual growth of others as we meet to fellowship, worship, serve, and learn together. Church membership brings glory to God. We are to be involved with other believers not just for our own benefit, but for the honor and glory of God. Robert Saucy wrote,

> Although the worshipper will be blessed in his own life through the experience of worship, the primary object of worship is not the subjective experience but the ascription of glory to God.

He continued, "To think in terms of how it lifted them up or 'gave them a good feeling' or 'inspired' is to substitute subjective affection for objective trust."[34] Ultimately, our participation in a church will bring honor to God.

---

[34] Saucy, 170.

The church in Acts grew as believers learned, worshiped, and shared together. Acts 2:46–47 tells us,

> So continuing daily with one accord in the temple, and breaking bread from house to house, they ate their food with gladness and simplicity of heart, praising God and having favor with all people. And the Lord added daily those who were being saved.

"The Lord" added to the church through the preaching of the Word, worship, and believers spreading the good news of the gospel. That pattern is the pattern that needs to be clearly demonstrated in a church today. Not man-centered efforts to attract or entertain, not marketing techniques, not programs, not calls to benevolence or social action, not fun social activities, but faithful presentation of the crucified and risen Christ. A good church is one whose members are equipped to live as ambassadors of their Lord Jesus Christ.

Find a church to attend. Don't just attend; join and become an active part of a group of believers seeking to honor and glorify God. Commit yourself to be a part of a church where there is a spirit of unity, and then add to that unity. As believers we share a common faith in Christ and have been reconciled to God through Him. There should be a strong sense of community, with role models and family models present in the congregation. There should be opportunity for fellowship and for development of friendships. Your church should be a place where you can look for support, safety, and comfort. It should be like a good family. We aren't left alone to live in isolation, but God has given us the church so we can learn and grow together, to serve and minister to each other.

Finally, remember that preferences are not absolutes. Style is not absolute. You likely will not find a church that does everything exactly the way you like, and you will need to be willing to compromise your preferences. Christ is honored when there is an observable oneness among His people. He is honored when we are a part of a community of believers with a shared sense of wonder and praise to the God who created and redeemed us for His honor and glory.

References

Chafer, Lewis Sperry, revised by Walvoord, John F. *Major Bible Themes*. Grand Rapids, Michigan: Zondervan Publishing House, 1976.

Dever, Mark. *Nine Marks of a Healthy Church*. Wheaton, Illinois: Crossway, 2013.

Leeman, Jonathan. *Word Centered Church*. Chicago, Illinois: Moody Publishers, 2017.

MacArthur, John Jr. *The Church the Body of Christ*. Grand Rapids, Michigan: Zondervan, 1973.

Manton, Thomas. *Works of Thomas Manton,* volume 1. Edinburgh, Scotland: Banner of Truth, 1993.

Saucy, Robert L. *The Church in God's Program*. Chicago, Illinois: Moody Press, 1972.

Schaeffer, Francis A. *The Great Evangelical Disaster*. Westchester, Illinois: Crossway Books, 1984.

Printed in the United States
By Bookmasters